B 543195

THE
REORGANIZATION OF THE OFFICE
OF
CHAMBERLAIN
1914

BY HENRY BRUÈRE
CHAMBERLAIN OF THE CITY OF NEW YORK

HJ
9289
.N44
A23
1915

THE REORGANIZATION
OF THE
OFFICE OF CHAMBERLAIN

1914

BY
HENRY BRUÈRE
CHAMBERLAIN
of the City of New York

PRESS OF
CLARENCE S. NATHAN, INC.
NEW YORK

CONTENTS

	Page
Letter of Transmittal	5
Legal Status of Chamberlain	10
Analysis of Functions	10
Receipt and Disbursement of Funds	11
Custody of City Funds	12
City Depositories	13
Test for Selection of Depositories	14
Interest on Deposits	14
Private Depositories Received Higher Rates of Interest than the City	15
City's Reserve	16
Rule for Making Deposits Formulated	16
Basis for Refusal to Designate a Bank as City Depository	17
Operation of New Rule for Distributing Deposits	18
Attitude of the Banks Towards New Rule	20
Surety Bonds for Deposits	21
Withdrawal of Deposits	22
Clearing and Collecting Accounts	23
Scattered Custody of City Funds	24
City Borrowing	24
Development of a Popular Market for City Bonds	27
Reducing Number of Depositories	28
Chamberlain as Trustee of Court Funds	29
Bond Investment of Trust Funds	33
Payment of Witnesses and Jurors	33
Bail Funds	34
Internal Reorganization	34
Routine and Regulations	36
Sinking Fund Commission – Its Merger with the Board of Estimate and Apportionment Recommended	37

282954

Hon. John Purroy Mitchel,
    Mayor, City of New York.
Sir:

The recent sale of $100,000,000 of corporate stock notes and revenue bonds to a syndicate of banks emphasizes a condition with respect to the city treasury which has for many years demanded consideration.

The chamberlain's office under the charter has exclusive jurisdiction over the deposit of funds in banks after their designation as city depositories by the banking commission. With balances ranging from $20,000,000 to $125,000,000, as they have during the past year, this power can be made of considerable moment in establishing proper credit relations for the city government.

The city borrows funds in anticipation of the collection of taxes and corporate stock sales on short term securities, and raises funds on long term bonds for public improvements. These loans have generally been made through private bankers or individual investors and only indirectly through the instrumentality of the banks of the city.

In the $100,000,000 issue of this year the comptroller called upon all the banks of New York to assist in floating the loan. Prior to this issue, in pursuance of a new policy of utilizing the investment market of England, France and Belgium to dispose of a part of the city's issues because of the great volume of New York City securities held in America, the comptroller had in 1914 made loans abroad totaling $80,000,000, falling due at various dates before January 1st, 1915. War conditions necessitated making provision for the settlement of these European loans by the payment of gold. To obtain gold to pay the loans, the coöperation of the various banks of the city was sought. This coöperation was secured through the agency of two private banking houses acting as syndicate managers. Under the arrangement planned by the syndicate managers all the banks of the city were called on to subscribe to the loan in an amount proportionate to their size, and to agree to pay at least 80 per cent. of their subscription in gold, if called upon to do so. In return for the loans, in addition to interest at the rate of 6 per cent. and an arrangement for the payment of a possible profit on exchange, it was agreed that the city should leave in the various subscribing banks the amount of their subscription, except as funds were needed to settle outstanding obligations. In view of the fact that 17 of the banks subscribing to the loan were not city depositories at the time of the sale, it was necessary for the banking commission specially to designate them as such.

Under this contract, therefore, with respect to the $100,000,000, the chamberlain's discretion in distributing funds among approved depositories was supplanted by the loan agreement.

My own judgment is that a working arrangement between banks as creditors in loaning money to the city and as debtors in receiving city deposits, somewhat along the lines of the arrangement effected in the $100,000,000 loan, should systematically be made. I have felt so from the beginning of my tenure of office. Under the charter the chamberlain has no jurisdiction whatsoever over loans, although he exclusively controls bank balances. So far as I know no definite agreement of a general character has ever been effected to correlate loans with deposits except in the case of this emergency. The comptroller has now under advisement, with the assurance of my heartiest coöperation, plans for making some permanent arrangement along these lines to the end that the deposits of the city may be correlated with its borrowings.

The problem of distributing city balances is in itself a considerable one, and has heretofore been based on the theory that they should be distributed as widely as possible, in view of the fact that they represent taxes paid by the various sections of the community and that the banks in the different localities are in turn called upon to provide accommodations for the taxpayers in their respective territories.

On taking office, I found that this practice as a general principle was further modified by the individual judgment of the chamberlain as to the amounts that should be placed in any particular bank. Under the very generous limitation that the law establishes, no bank may receive a city deposit in excess of 50 per cent. of its capital and surplus.

In order to substitute some definite principle of distribution of deposits for the uncertain discretion of a single official, which it is impossible to exercise wisely with reference to the more than 100 institutions which serve as depositories, I determined to place deposits in banks according to the size and strength of the bank and the rate of interest paid on daily balances by the bank in question. This policy resulted in the payment of considerably higher interest rates on bank balances, due to equalizing the rate paid on city balances with the rate paid on commercial and private balances, as the law requires. The increase above interest earnings in other years, due to this new method of making deposits, aggregated, for the 11 months during which the plan was in operation in 1914, $114,041, or twice the total cost of my office for that year.

Though satisfactory in this respect, the plan, from the standpoint of credit arrangements, is obviously merely a make-shift. There should be established some definite, permanent basis of credit relationship between banks serving as city depositories and the city.* The city will for some time to come continue to borrow for current needs because it cannot time the collection of its income with the necessary routine of its expenditures. To make its borrowings advantageously the municipality finds it necessary, in times of emergency, to deal with the banks of deposit. The comptroller, who now has complete authority over borrowing, should, in my judgment, exercise an equal authority over the distribution of city deposits. I believe further, as a matter of sound public and business administration, that this

---

* See page 26 for description of loan and deposit arrangements between the city of Buffalo and its depository banks.

authority to make loans should be qualified by the requirement that the mayor or board of estimate give approval to arrangements entered into by the comptroller. The comptroller should, nevertheless, have a free hand in utilizing the resources of the city in establishing favorable credit relations, and city deposits can be made a potent factor in making satisfactory credit arrangements.

This being the case, unless recommendations made by various charter commissions in recent years looking to widening the functions of the chamberlain's office be adopted, there does not seem to me to be adequate reason for continuing the office of chamberlain as such. At present, the principal charter function of the chamberlain is the custody of city funds. Other duties such as trustee of court funds, custodian of military funds, and the receipt and custody of cash bail, might easily be discharged by a subordinate official of the department of finance.

My recommendation is that either the chamberlain's office be made a genuine department of the city treasury to which there be assigned, as provided by the Ivins and Gaynor charters, the duty of collecting city funds as well as their safe-keeping, or that it be merged with the department of finance. There is no logic in the present arrangement whereby water revenues are collected by the water department, license fees by the department of licenses, taxes and assessments by the comptroller, and permit fees by a host of bureaus and offices responsible to the various elective officials. Good administration demands that there be one central collection office for all city revenues, as every recent charter commission after a study has recommended. Whether this centralization should be placed under the mayor or under the comptroller is, no doubt, a debatable question.

Briefly, my own view is as follows: The department of finance is the fiscal agency for the city government. My mature judgment after many years of study of the question is that it is wise to vest in that department, properly controlled, responsibility for all fiscal functions. The growth of the administrative departments of the city commits to the mayor so many questions of administration and operation, that a coördinate official should have peculiar responsibility for the proper performance of the city's fiscal operations.

It may be suggested that the comptroller should not have power to audit disbursements and to make them too, and for this reason the city treasury should be maintained as a separate establishment. But the comptroller may make no payments now without the approval of the mayor, given in routine course by affixing the signature of the mayor's chief clerk to warrants drawn on the chamberlain.

Under the charter the commissioners of accounts must audit all receipts and disbursements. In practice the audit both of warrants and vouchers audited by the comptroller is made after disbursement. The commissioners of accounts' audit of vouchers could feasibly be made before disbursement, thus checking in advance of payment the authority for payment, and verifying after payment the fact of disbursement. As much protection as is now afforded by the power of the chamberlain to withhold payment would be afforded by the power of the mayor to withhold his approval of the payment. In other words, with the mayor and the commissioners of accounts to check the comptroller's disbursements, and the more exact control over all financial transactions that now prevails as the result of the recent reorganization of the city's accounting practices, the additional check of the independent treasury is no longer required.

This recommendation is not made with the thought that any material economies will be effected by abolishing the title of chamberlain. On the contrary, there may be an actual increase of current expenditure if this recommendation is carried out. In the first place, the clerical and administrative work done in the chamberlain's office must be continued even though the work is transferred to the department of finance. I have reduced the working force to a minimum. There will be a saving of the chamberlain's salary. Offsetting this will be the loss of added interest earnings many times this amount which will result, if the present policy of placing deposits at rates higher than 2 per cent. is partly superseded by a credit arrangement basis, as herein discussed. This credit arrangement will be in the form of insurance against a disadvantageous borrowing market. On the other hand, years may pass before the city finds itself again in a position where it is compelled to rely on the depository banks for loans. The change, therefore, is recommended with a view toward a better administrative arrangement and not to accomplish some petty economy as several misinformed taxpayers' organizations have mistakenly supposed.

I have several times discussed this proposal with you and understand that you regard it desirable to defer the reorganization herein recommended until the contemplated revised charter is prepared. This will doubtless be wise inasmuch as piecemeal charter revision will only further complicate the important task of charter simplification that is so much needed. The readjustment of the city treasury is only one of many desirable, radical alterations in the present organization of the city government.

Some currency has been given to the statement that the chamberlain's office is useless. This, of course, is absurd. The functions of the chamberlain, as such, are of the greatest importance involving as they do the custody of the city's cash and the management of important trusts. The question is merely whether a more businesslike arrangement will result from consolidating these functions with the other fiscal functions of the city.

I do not take into consideration, in making this recommendation, the marked broadening of the duties of the chamberlain along administrative lines which has resulted from your utilization of this office during your term for general administrative work. Such work as during the past year I have performed for you in an administrative capacity, assisting you in a multitude of administrative questions which the mayor must deal with if he is to be effectively in touch with the work for which he is responsible, should be performed by a commissioner of administration, whose establishment I recommended at the beginning of 1914. Such an office should be an instrument of day by day assistance to the mayor in the performance of his work as general manager of the city government, which he must increasingly become. More and more the city of New York, if it is to be well-governed, should develop towards the city manager plan. It is already a fact that the public looks to the mayor for the proper performance of all public service. His mind, therefore, should be free from responsibility for the ways and means of financing the city, and his energies fully reserved for intimate and consecutive attention to the problems of operation and constructive development.*

In the report which follows I have discussed the various problems involved in administering the chamberlain's office, which are in themselves of considerable consequence. It has been my task during my term to deal with an aggravated situation with respect to mortgage investments held by the chamberlain as trustee for various court funds. The policy that I have pursued in regard to these investments is fully discussed in this report.

By readjustment of the work of the office I have cut down its annual cost, and shall be able to turn it over, I trust, in satisfactory working condition. I wish to say emphatically that great credit is due to the energy and interest devoted to the work of this office during the past year by members of the staff and by my deputy, Mr. George L. Bergen. The public must not entertain the idea that there is no work for the employees of this office. On the contrary, the care of deposits aggregating from $20,000,000 to upwards of $125,000,000, the approval of warrants and the handling of trust funds give to the office a volume of work quite equal to the duties imposed on any staff of similar size in the city government.

Respectfully submitted,
HENRY BRUÈRE,
Chamberlain.

May 1, 1915.

---

* See special report on general administrative work assigned to the Chamberlain in the year 1914, to be issued June 1, 1915.

THE REORGANIZATION OF THE OFFICE OF CHAMBERLAIN OF THE CITY OF NEW YORK

Legal Status of Chamberlain

The office of the chamberlain is by law a bureau of the department of finance. The chamberlain, however, is appointed by the mayor and is removable by him. His principal function is the custodianship of public funds paid into the city treasury, and in this respect his duties correspond to those of a customary city treasurer. By law, and as a matter of fact, the chamberlain performs as well the functions of county treasurer for the five counties comprised within the city of New York.

The salary of the chamberlain is fixed by charter at $12,000 a year. Prior to 1898 the office was a fee office of lucrative emoluments.

Analysis of Functions

Except for those who come to deposit or to withdraw cash bail in criminal and civil cases, jurors and witnesses who come to claim their checks, and those who come to pay in or withdraw funds which the chamberlain holds in trust under court orders, the chamberlain's office has no contact with the public.

It has so happened that during previous administrations, in the work of reorganizing the business of the city, the office of the chamberlain had not been included. Little was known of it by the general public, and in the general reorganization of the department of finance the practices and methods of the bureau of the city treasury had not been materially affected.

To bring the office into harmony with the new methods of city administration latterly put in force in New York City departments, it was first necessary to obtain a record of its functions and the work it is called upon to perform, together with the manner of its performance. No such record was available. There were books of accounts, there were office practices, and there were statutes and habits of generations, but there were no directions, no procedures, no regulations formulated by administrative authority to govern the operation of the office.

Facts regarding the methods of the office were obtained with the courteous help of my predecessor, Mr. Robert R. Moore, and from the various employees, many of whom are exceptionally well informed on the powers and duties of the office, the exercise of which is delegated to them.

Beginning on January 2d, 1914, step by step, I made personally an analysis of each process and record of the office. In order that I might gain perspective on the business of the office, I obtained a staff of examiners from the commissioners of accounts to assist me in a thorough investigation of every process and to trace back the transactions of the office for a period of years. This examination showed that there were two principal problems to be dealt with: (1) the problem of the receipt and disbursement of city funds involving the proper handling of bank balances and the city's relationship with various banks serving as city depositories, and (2) the proper custody and investment of trust funds committed to the chamberlain by the courts. Other problems of bookkeeping, office devices, simplification of methods, adjustment of personnel, and the enforcement of economies, all group themselves about these two major questions.

Receipt and Disbursement of Funds

In respect of the receipt and disbursement of city funds the chamberlain's functions are purely ministerial. If they were not so, the work would be a duplication of the work of the comptroller who is the auditor general of the city government.

The charter prohibits the payment by the chamberlain of funds out of the city treasury, unless there is a sufficient balance in the specific appropriation or fund affected to meet the payment. For years the chamberlain had kept memorandum records of drafts on the various funds and appropriations for the purpose of preventing payments not authorized by law. While these records were kept in the chamberlain's bureau, there had been effected a complete reorganization of the accounting methods of the department of finance, practically making impossible an overdraft on a fund or appropriation. After referring the legality of the proposal to discontinue these records to the corporation counsel, and obtaining his approval, an arrangement was made with the comptroller whereby the chamberlain now accepts a special certificate of the department of finance placed on the warrant as security that the draft in question is within the limits of the fund to which it applies. This made possible the elimination of five warrant clerkships. Three of the incumbents, in service for a number of years, were, through the comptroller's courtesy, transferred to vacancies in the department of finance.

As a part of the procedure of disbursing funds, the mayor is required to approve warrants prior to their payment, and the commissioners of accounts to audit them after the disbursement is made. The mayor's approval is affixed by the chief clerk of the mayor's office. I found that in the mayor's office an elaborate procedure had been developed to check warrants and warrant schedules to prevent errors in the payment of amounts drawn by the department of finance. There existed, therefore, three checks on city disbursements before payment,—the auditor's office in the department of finance, where the warrants are drawn and where all mistakes should be detected, the mayor's office, and finally the chamberlain's office.

The approval of the mayor affords a theoretical check on payments and should be continued, especially if the chamberlain's office is consolidated with the department of finance. But it was not necessary, and will not be in the future, for the mayor's office to maintain records and a staff of clerks to duplicate work already done and which should be done with complete accuracy in the department of finance. Consequently, we have eliminated some of the unnecessary work performed by the mayor's chief clerk, and as a step in the direction of combining the mayor's check with the check of the commissioners of accounts, have transferred the mayor's warrant clerks from the City Hall to the Municipal Building, where they are under the supervision of the commissioners of accounts. Incidentally, this makes it unnecessary to carry from the Municipal Building to the City Hall and back again the hundreds of warrants which are drawn each day. Receipts on account of city funds come into the custody of the chamberlain through their deposit by collecting offices in designated depository banks or by payment directly to this office.

As county treasurer, the chamberlain, for the five counties comprising the city of New York, receives pursuant to court order:

1—Deposits made to satisfy mechanics' liens.
2—Proceeds of foreclosure of mortgages, known as surplus monies.
3—Proceeds of sales of infants' real estate.
4—Proceeds of partition actions.
5—Funds involved in Surrogates' Court proceedings.
6—Bail funds deposited in criminal and civil actions.
7—Tenders before trial.
8—Security for costs.

All receipts and disbursements of the foregoing funds are made pursuant to specific court orders, and involve no discretion on the part of the chamberlain, unless the order as drawn does not comply with court rules. This occurs very frequently. The funds must either be deposited in banks designated by the state comptroller or invested in New York state or city bonds.*

Custody of City Funds

During the course of the year there comes into the city treasury upwards of $700,000,000, a sum which has increased over $300,000,000 in the past ten years. Actual collections are made in the first instance by the various bureaus and departments of the city, and are received by the chamberlain when the collecting bureaus deposit their collections to the credit of the city in one of the designated depositories. In some instances they pay the actual cash to the chamberlain. Once this money is paid into the city treasury, the chamberlain is solely responsible for its safe-keeping. It is obligatory, of course, to deposit receipts in banks selected by the banking commission, of which he is a member, but how much is to be placed in each depository and

---

* Formerly investments in mortgages were permitted. This was prohibited in 1911 because of improper investments. See p. 29.

from which particular depository withdrawals are to be made, are wholly* within his discretion, except that under the charter the deposit in a particular bank may not exceed 50 per cent. of its capital and surplus.

City Depositories

Depositories are selected quarterly by the banking commission consisting of the mayor, the comptroller and the chamberlain. Practically every well established bank and trust company in the city is a depository except a few of the smaller institutions in the outlying boroughs and one or two banks that decline to pay interest. Banks designated as city depositories commonly advertise as a business asset the fact of their service as a depository.

On January 1st, 1914, on my taking office, there were 107 banks in the five boroughs of the city designated as city depositories by the banking commission. The average total balance in these banks for the year 1913 was $35,939,824. The capital, surplus and undivided profits of the banks serving as city depositories ranged from $125,000 to $57,000,000. The balances in individual banks during the year, exclusive of the clearing accounts into which collections are paid and from which disbursements are made, range from $25,000 to $4,000,000.

Obviously, the city is an important client of the banking institutions of New York. A corporation carrying balances averaging over $35,000,000 has a valuable business which is of great commercial banking importance.

The city of New York is the largest city borrower in the world, for its borrowings, made up, in part, of loans for days, weeks or months, reborrowed many times throughout the year in anticipation of tax and other revenue collections, exceeded $550,000,000 in 1913. But it is also a great lender of money, the total of its loans exceeding $700,000,000 in a single year. These loans are made to the banks in the form of deposits.

So here is a considerable power, easily abused and one whose abuse can be made profitable to favored institutions. We sought to learn, therefore, what principle, if any, had governed the chamberlain's office in making deposits in banks, and what information was on file in the office respecting the character of the banks with which deposits were currently kept. No principle was found except that the general policy existed of placing substantial deposits in larger institutions and distributing small deposits as widely as possible among the lesser banks of the city. The amounts of deposits and the period of their retention in a particular bank were governed by the personal judgment of the chamberlain, and were often, no doubt, the subject of personal or political considerations. It is true that the main clearing account was kept in the largest bank in the city, and that this bank, empowered under the law to loan $5,000,000 to a single borrower customarily loaned the city large amounts during the course of the year, the total of these loans in 1913 being over $78,000,000. But balances, withdrawals and deposits in other depositories seemed to have been governed solely

---

* This power was restricted, with respect to a particular transaction, in the recent bond sale in which the comptroller agreed to retain the amounts of the sale of notes and bonds purchased by the several subscribing banks as a deposit in the respective banks, until the cash was needed for the redemption of the foreign loans.

by the chamberlain's judgment. It was found, in addition, that in each of the five boroughs comprising the city a bank had been selected to receive deposits from officials collecting city funds.

An analysis was made running back to the year 1909 of the average daily balances kept in each bank. It was found that some banks maintained a practically even balance, while other banks had deposits for a time and then were without them, thus creating foundation for the assertion frequently made that city deposits were less desirable than other classes of deposit because they were liable to sudden and complete withdrawal.

Test for Selection of Depositories

The first consideration in depositing city funds is to put them in a safe bank. To indicate their strength and soundness, banks publish statements of their condition.

Obviously, it is impossible for any single official to deal with equal justice with over 100 banks unless those dealings are based upon some principle, governed by the advantages and disadvantages to the city which result from such dealings. No single individual can have personal information regarding the character of 100 banks, information which is laboriously obtained by state and national bank examiners, unless that information is systematically collected and systematically recorded.

It is quite impossible to determine precisely, by means of these published statements, the comparative strength of the various banks. The coöperation of state and national bank examiners was, therefore, requested on the ground that the city, as a public institution, should have available to it information as precise as possible on the condition of the banks with which it dealt. The importance of this caution was emphasized by the fact that the city is now carrying in defunct banks upwards of $490,000.

It is a business commonplace that the strength of a bank is measurably indicated by the ratio of its capital and surplus to its deposits. I determined, therefore, to grade the banks according to this ratio.

Interest on Deposits

By charter requirement, city funds placed in depositories must be credited with interest. Prior to this administration the city received two per cent. on daily balances from city depositories. These balances were treated by the depositories in this respect as the reserves of country banks were treated by the metropolitan banks. Moreover, there was a general theory that this rate of interest was adequate for a depositor so continuously a borrower as the city and so likely to make arbitrary withdrawals of its deposits. The charter requires that the banking commission fix the rate of interest quarterly, and in accordance with the prevailing rate paid by banks on similar accounts to firms and individuals. The precise language of the charter is:

Sec. 196. "* * * * * * no such bank or trust company shall be designated unless its various officers shall agree to pay into the city treasury interest on the daily balances at a rate to be fixed by the mayor and the chamberlain and the said comptroller of the city of New York, by a majority vote, which rate shall be so fixed quarterly on the first days of February, May, August and November in each year, according to the current rate of interest upon like balances deposited in banks and trust companies in the city of New York by *private persons or corporations.*"

Accordingly, it has been for many years the practice of the chamberlain to issue an invitation to banks each quarter requesting from them proposals on the rate of interest to be paid during the following quarter. The proposals seldom varied. Year after year and quarter after quarter replies were made that interest at the rate of 2 per cent. would be paid. On January 1st, 1914, I found that 102 depository banks paid 2 per cent., 3 banks paid $2\frac{1}{2}$ per cent. and 2 banks 3 per cent.

It is important to state here in explanation of one of the reasons for the payment of lower rates of interest on city deposits, that the law does not permit the city to make time deposit arrangements with banks. It therefore cannot stipulate that balances will be kept in any amount for any fixed period. This makes it necessary for the bank to loan funds obtained through city deposits practically as demand money, that is, subject to call. They are also obliged, under the law, to maintain a larger reserve on this class of deposits than on time deposits.

Private Depositors Received Higher Rates of Interest than the City

It was found on inquiry that certain banks were paying to private depositors rates of interest in excess of those paid by them on city deposits, and that in one or two instances they were paying higher rates of interest on comparatively small accounts kept with them by one department or another of the city government than they paid on the very much larger deposits maintained with them by the chamberlain. A certain national bank paid $2\frac{1}{2}$ per cent. interest to a department on a balance of $7,500, while paying the city 2 per cent. on balances ranging from $50,000 to $100,000.

With the five minor exceptions referred to previously, 2 per cent. was the prevailing rate paid on city balances. The requirement of the charter was disregarded and the issuance of the quarterly invitation had become a perfunctory routine. It was the crystallized custom of years that irrespective of all variations in the value of money, irrespective of the size or continuance of balances, 2 per cent. was to be paid on city balances. It is not argued that 2 per cent. is too low, nor that the city should seek to earn interest on its balances as a primary consideration in selecting depositories for its funds. But it seemed to me unquestionable that rates of interest received by the city on its funds should, with proper regard to safety, be made to conform, as the charter requires, to rates paid on similar balances of "private persons or corporations." Accordingly, I proceeded on that assumption.

City's Reserve

In order to establish a direct relationship between the city and each individual bank desiring to serve as a depository, and to base the interest quotations upon the practice and ability of the bank to pay interest, a statement was prepared for each bank showing, for a period of five years, the amount of the city's balance in the bank in question. In addition, a plan to control deposits was outlined which would substitute reasonable system for chance or whim in the city's withdrawals of its balances. I found that certain banks enjoyed practically permanent balances but that these banks made no correspondingly increased return to the city. The problem was to obtain for the city an appropriate return for comparative stability of deposits, if stability could be obtained. How this was done will be shown below.

An examination of the past transactions of the office showed that as a requirement of good business method, the city maintained on deposit in the banks a minimum average daily balance of $20,000,000. This minimum balance averaged approximately twice the amount of the warrants outstanding against the city treasury at any particular time. For some time a balance of this amount has remained intact from one year's end to another, being replenished from time to time through borrowing in accordance with the fluctuations in the receipt of taxes and other revenues and in payments from the city treasury. During the year this balance had twice been greatly increased, first, through the sale, because of an advantageous market, of $60,000,000 in corporate stock early in April in advance of maturity of corporate stock notes, and second, by reason of the $100,000,000 sale in the fall. Balances in 1914 were, therefore, extraordinarily high.

In order to maintain a suitable balance in the clearing account, not too high, nor too low for safety, painstaking effort has been made to keep advised of prospective large payments. This is not always easy because there is no means of anticipating large contract payments. Redemptions of loans are now reported a month in advance so that the chamberlain may make timely provision for them in the drawing or clearing account. These practices have resulted from a closer relationship between the department of finance and the office of the chamberlain.

Rule for Making Deposits Formulated

It was obvious, therefore, that the city would always retain in the banks a very considerable sum as a matter of simple business precaution. This fact furnished the basis for a proposal to the banks, namely, that deposits on which higher rates of interest were offered would be left intact so long as there were funds available in the balances on which lower rates of interest were paid. This proposal of itself seemed subject to the possible criticism that the city would disregard the strength of the bank in making deposits in order to obtain a higher rate of interest, and thus jeopardize public funds. No bank of questionable security should be accepted by the city as a depository under any circumstances. Therefore, the banks were notified that a maximum limit would be placed on all deposits of 20 per cent. of capital and surplus instead of the 50 per cent. authorized by law, and that within this 20 per cent. a further limitation would be placed in accordance with the ratio of the total deposits in a particular institution to its combined capital and surplus. The rule finally worked out was stated in the quarterly notice to banks issued prior to the interest fixing day, August 1st. At that time the six months operation of the rule had led to one or two minor adjustments of the plan as first formulated. These are not of sufficient significance to merit discussion. The rule follows:

> "A definite maximum of 20 per cent. of the combined capital and surplus is placed on the amount that may be deposited in any bank. In determining this maximum a basis of 10 per cent. of the combined capital and surplus of the bank is taken. For every additional $\frac{1}{4}$ per cent. of interest paid on daily balances over 2 per cent. an additional $2\frac{1}{2}$ per cent. of the capital and surplus of the bank is added, up to the maximum of 20 per cent. From the total amount which may be placed in any bank on this basis, deductions are made at the rate of $\frac{1}{2}$ per cent. of capital and surplus for every unit of variation above the ratio of five to one between deposits in that particular bank and its total capital and surplus."

Basis for Refusal to Designate a Bank as City Depository

Banks are trustworthy according to the discretion, honesty and ability of their managers. There are certain practices so obviously wrong, in that they jeopardize the interest of depositors, that banks are prohibited by statute from practicing them. There are other practices and requirements deemed essential to good banking and these in turn are demanded of banks by state or national laws. To secure the enforcement of all these laws periodic examinations of state and national banks are made by state and national bank examiners, respectively. In this way the interest of depositors is measurably protected. But the real and substantial protection of depositors is found in the character of a bank's managers.

In the banks and trust companies serving as depositories for the city there are 1,500 different directors. Obviously, it is impossible for any one to have personal acquaintance directly or indirectly with the business character of so many individuals. At least the present chamberlain has not the acquaintance. Obviously, too, a number of the larger institutions may safely be assumed to be sound, and many though of smaller size have demonstrated their soundness by years of successful operation. But there are banks of purely local reputation that persistently seek to serve as depositories and there are other banks concerning which there are from time to time vague rumors of which a public official must take heed. To obtain as precise information as possible of the condition of all banks, I have reviewed the condition of the state banks with the state superintendent of banks, and of the national banks with the national bank examiner. Supplementing this, I have kept up-to-date a detailed statement of the condition of each bank. This is before me at all times and is used as a guide in selecting depositories and in controlling balances.

In several instances I have recommended that banks be not designated depositories because they were too recently established. In another instance I declined to place a deposit in a certain bank because I was informed that it carried excessive loans based on real estate security, in other words, that its resources were not in suitably liquid form. In each such case the basis for my action has been freely discussed with the bank affected and my objections have been withdrawn when evidence of a properly sound condition was presented. In every instance the bank affected has been most candid in furnishing such information.

In other instances I have carefully restricted deposits in certain banks within sums covered by suitable surety because of the character of its depositors. It does not seem proper to me that unsecured public funds should be placed in any institution susceptible to easily stimulated runs.

The mental anxiety which one experiences, when responsible for some hundred odd separate bank accounts, all of substantial sums, makes it plain that there cannot be too much public supervision of banking institutions, nor too much publicity given to banking transactions.

Operation of New Rule for Distributing Deposits

During the days immediately preceding February 1st, 1914, the first quarterly interest fixing date occurring in this administration, a number of representatives of banks called at the chamberlain's office to discuss the question of city deposits. The general purpose of these calls seemed to be to establish business relations, and in some instances frankly to solicit the deposits of the city. To each of these callers the statement was made that the chamberlain would regard the selection of city depositories entirely impersonally, and would make these selections on the basis of facts regarding the conditions of the banks in question obtained from reliable and authoritative sources.

At this time money was exceptionally plentiful and interest rates unusually low. Banks generally had an excess of deposits and were making comparatively few loans. In other words, there was no general demand for increased deposits. Despite this extremely "soft" condition of the money market, in response to an individual letter, 54 banks and trust companies with a combined capital and surplus of $186,199,000, submitted offers to pay $2\frac{1}{2}$ per cent. or better on current balances. In these banks, under the rule adopted and previously explained, it was possible to deposit $27,000,000.

The following is an example of the letter sent to the banks:

OFFICE OF THE CHAMBERLAIN

City Depositories, Designated February 1, 1915

STATEMENT OF BALANCES AT CLOSE OF BUSINESS, ..., 1915.

NATIONAL BANKS	Rate Paid	Balance	STATE BANKS	Rate Paid	Balance	TRUST COMPANIES	Rate Paid	Balance
Borough of Manhattan			**Borough of Manhattan**			**Borough of Manhattan**		
American Exchange			America			Astor		
Bank of N. Y., N. B. A.			Bowery			Bankers'		
Battery Park			Broadway-Central			Broadway		
Butchers' & Drovers'			Bryant Park			Central		
Chase			Century			Columbia		
Chatham & Phenix			Chelsea Exchange			Commercial		
Citizens' Central			Colonial			Empire		
City (Active)			Columbia			Equitable		
Coal & Iron			Corn Exchange			Farmers' Loan		
Commerce			Corn Exchange (Washington Branch)			Fidelity		
East River						Fulton		
Fifth			German-American			Guaranty		
First			German Exchange			Hudson		
Garfield			Germania			Lawyers' Title Ins		
Gotham			Greenwich			Lincoln		
Hanover			Manhattan Co.			Metropolitan		
Harriman			Metropolis			New York		
Importers' & Traders'			Metropolitan			N. Y. Life Ins		
Irving			Mutual			Transatlantic		
Liberty			New Netherland			Union		
Lincoln			N. Y. Prod. Exch.			United States		
Market & Fulton			Pacific			U. S. Mortgage		
Mechanics & Metals			Public					
Merchants'			Security			**Borough of Brooklyn**		
Merchants' Exchange			State			Brooklyn		
N. Y. County			United States			Franklin		
Park			Washington Heights			Hamilton		
Second			West Side			Kings Co. (Inactive)		
Union Exchange			Yorkville			Kings County (Active)		
						Mfctrs.-Citizens'		
Borough of Brooklyn			**Borough of Brooklyn**			People's (Inactive)		
City (Inactive)			Coney Island			People's (Active)		
City (Active)			Flatbush			Title Guarantee		
First			Mechanics'					
Greenpoint			Montauk			**Borough of Queens**		
Nassau			North Side			Queens County		
People's								
Ridgewood			**Borough of Queens**			Northern Bank		
			Corn Exch. (Active)			Carnegie Trust Co.		
Borough of Queens			Hillside					
First of Corona			Long Island			Total		
First of Jamaica								
			Borough of Richmond			City Treasury		
Borough of The Bronx			Corn Exch. (Active)			S'k'g Fund Redemption		
Bronx						S'k'g Fund Interest		
			Borough of The Bronx			S'k'g Fund Redemption No. 2		
			Bronx Borough			S'k'g Fund, City of New York		
			Corn Exch. (Active)			S'k'g Fund, City of Brooklyn		
			Cosmopolitan			S'k'g Fund, L.I.C., Red. Fire Bonds		
			Twenty-third Ward			S'k'g Fund, L.I.C., Red. Water Bonds		
			Westchester Ave			Water S'k'g Fd., City of N. Y.		
						Water S'k'g Fd., City of Brooklyn		
						Interest Registered		
						Unclaimed Interest		
						Jury Fees		
						Witness Fees		
						Redemption of Coupon Bonds		
						Total		

"Pursuant to a provision of law, the banking commission, consisting of the mayor, comptroller and chamberlain, will meet on February 2d, 1914, to select depositories for city funds and to fix the rate of interest for the three months ending April 30, 1914.

"As you are aware, it is the practice of the city to carry from $20,000,000 to $30,000,000 in cash in active and inactive accounts. Under a plan that has been in vogue for many years, there are at present a single clearing account and several other active accounts of smaller amount. There are about one hundred additional depositories where funds are maintained practically inactive, drafts being made only when it is necessary to replenish the clearing account. In a sense, a considerable portion of these inactive balances is carried as a reserve against an insufficiency of current receipts to meet current expenditures.

"During the past four years your average daily balance has ranged from $450,000 to $800,000.

"It seems reasonable to expect from the inactive accounts a higher rate of interest than from the active accounts, where banks render a larger degree of service. Of course, it is impossible to assure you of any fixed balance for any definite term. I desire to inquire, however, under these conditions, what rate of interest you would pay if you are designated a city depository for the next three months? If you will pay different rates for different amounts, kindly indicate the amounts, at such rates, that you care to receive. I may assure you that assuming the bank to be of proper strength and under safe and conservative management, I shall take under consideration the rates of interest paid in making transfers to the clearing account."

On the next quarterly interest fixing day occurring May 1st, 71 banks and trust companies, with a combined capital and surplus of $178,095,000, agreed to pay $2\frac{1}{4}$ per cent. or better. On August 1st, at the outbreak of the European war with its disturbance of the money market, 82 banks and trust companies, with a combined capital and surplus of $285,893,000, agreed to pay $2\frac{1}{2}$ per cent. or better. In November, although the war conditions were then in an acute stage, 91 banks and trust companies, with a combined capital and surplus of $336,479,000, agreed to pay $2\frac{1}{2}$ per cent. or better. Thus with each quarter the number of banks offering higher rates of interest increased.

Prior to August 1st the strengthening of the money market in part accounted for the growing demand for city deposits at favorable rates of interest. But a further and important reason was the demonstration made from month to month that the announced rule would be strictly complied with. There were no sudden and arbitrary withdrawals from depositories. Withdrawals were made in proportional amount from all members of a class of banks and advance notice was given of the city's intention to make a substantial withdrawal.

Attitude of the Banks Towards New Rule

There is a very definite conviction among many bankers, particularly those operating under national charters, that 2 per cent. is the maximum interest, consistent with sound banking, that should be paid on deposits. There is also very justifiable objection to the city's attempting to increase interest rates by stimulating competition among banks for city deposits. With this latter view I entirely sympathize, and accordingly I sought to avoid competition, and announced that I was not so much interested in the rate of interest paid as in the soundness of the bank and the equitableness of the rule under which deposits were placed.

In order to obtain as many suggestions as possible from practical bankers, depositories were specifically requested to offer suggestions for the modification and improvement of the rule promulgated. All replies received except one were in the form of emphatic expressions in favor of the new plan. This one banker suggested that the principle adopted was wrong and that the rate of interest should be fixed in accordance with the prevailing rate for call money, since city deposits, he argued, were practically usable by the banks only for call money purposes. This plan, however, did not seem feasible, and was apparently inadmissible under the requirements of the charter. I quote here comments on the plan of distribution of deposits made by a number of the largest institutions in the city:

"I have no criticism to offer in relation to the plan."

"We are glad to see this worked out on a systematic basis."

". . . . which meets with our approval, as it seems to be an equitable method for the distribution of the city deposits."

". . . . and which we think are satisfactory in every respect."

"Very businesslike way . . . . fair to every institution in the city, and I can see no reason for anyone to make any complaint."

"We believe this is good business for the city of New York, is based on scientific principles and it is fair for all concerned."

"We think the plan a very equitable one."

". . . . and think the plan as outlined is a good one."

"We certainly cannot see anything to criticise in your plan. On the contrary, from every standpoint, it seems to be fair and equitable to the depositories and beneficial to the city's interest."

"The method seems to us very fair and reasonable and meets with our approval."

Other comments, similar to the above, are on file in the chamberlain's office. These expressions do not mean, of course, that the plan prepared is the best devisable, but they indicate with convincing emphasis that whatever the plan, to meet with the candid approval of business men, it must be based on some clear, announced principle and not on patronage or personal considerations.

All this clarification of an important branch of the city's business was in process when the European war broke out, disarranging the city's credit arrangements and leading to a general subscription to a temporary bond issue by all the banks of the city. This loan was made in lieu of the day by day borrowings customarily made to meet the maturing obligations of the city, and under an arrangement made by the syndicate managers the amount of each bank's subscription was immediately redeposited with it. For the remainder of the year 1914 the major part of the city's funds was banked according to the arrangement made by the banking syndicate and not according to the plan herein described and in operation since February 1st. The significant features of the syndicate arrangement, in so far as they affected city deposits, were:

1—The correlation of loans with deposits (as they should be correlated).

2—The substitution of a loan agreement executed by the comptroller with the bankers for the discretion of the chamberlain in the distribution of the funds among the banks.

3—The designation of banks as depositories because of their subscription to the loan.

4—Subordination of the payment of interest to credit accommodation. (A number of the banks which received 6 per cent. on the money loaned to the city were also at the time of the loan paying $2\frac{1}{2}$ per cent. or 3 per cent. on regular city deposits. On the funds loaned by them to the city, and remaining on deposit with them they paid 2 per cent. The city had in certain banks, during the period in which the emergency loan funds were kept in banks, a regular deposit bearing interest at $2\frac{1}{2}$ per cent. or 3 per cent. and a special deposit bearing 2 per cent. interest.)

Surety Bonds for Deposits

Chicago requires all banks serving as depositories to furnish surety bonds in the amount of their deposits. Personal sureties are accepted. In 1911, after the Carnegie Trust Company and Northern Trust Company failures, involving city deposits, a law was passed requiring the city to demand surety bonds from banks carrying inactive accounts. This provision has not been operative under the theory that the city has no inactive accounts inasmuch as all are subject to withdrawal at any time.

On January 1st, 1914, there were 10 banks serving as city depositories from which bonds were required. This number has been increased to 15. With one exception, these securities consist of city bonds deposited with the city under a contingent assignment. City funds should not be placed in any bank of whose solvency there is the slightest question. It may seem wise under special circumstances to require security for deposits, though as a business principle careful observation of the condition of the banks serving as depositories and selection of only the soundest banks in the first instance should be ample protection. There is no more reason for the city demanding security for its deposits than for private depositors demanding security for theirs. If proper care is exercised in selecting depositories and in restricting deposits to conservative limits (as, for example, the 20 per cent. limitation now in force on city deposits), the general responsibility of the banks may be accepted as adequate security for the safety of deposits.

Withdrawal of Deposits

The present practice in making withdrawals from the depository banks to the clearing account is to give telephonic notice, as far as possible, several days in advance of proposed withdrawals in order that if necessary the banks may recall loans and be prepared to facilitate payment. Not infrequently, where special request is made by the bank for longer notice, the time is extended, so that all appearance of arbitrariness is removed. This notice the banks are known to appreciate, and is an effective means for establishing friendly working relationships between the institutions and the city.

Under a haphazard plan where withdrawals are based upon the day by day judgment of the chamberlain without reference to any system, a bank is continuously exposed to punitive action in the form of arbitrary withdrawals which might seriously embarrass it in the routine performance of its business. The present rules make this impossible, because they require that withdrawal of any particular amount required be made pro rata among banks in the class to be affected. The classes consist of groups according to rates of interest paid. A deposit, no matter how large, is of slight value to a bank unless it has reasonable assurance of its retention for a sufficient period to enable it to loan the money advantageously and thus make a profit on the transaction.*

It is apparently impossible for the city accurately to forecast its total cash requirements from day to day, week to week or month to month. Payroll disbursements, with reasonable accuracy, can be anticipated and the cash arrangements accordingly made. Payments on account of contracts or current supply expenditures cannot be forecast, for there is no fixed rate of expenditure, nor any definitely determined period required for the audit and payment of the claim after it is filed with the contracting department.

The analyzed experience of 1914 shows that the average daily disbursements were approximately $2,000,000, but these may vary from time to time to amounts as much as $18,000,000. This condition which, in its exaggerated form leads to complete confusion in the handling of the city's cash, can be greatly minimized by close cooperation between the bookkeeping department of the comptroller's office and the chamberlain. I found, on taking office, that the daily reports of the comptroller of cash transactions and warrant action were not received by the chamberlain, and were, there-

---

*This fact furnishes an argument in favor of the reduction in the number of depositories, so that balances maintained in them may be of a sufficiently substantial character to make the business attractive and to establish a basis for reciprocity between the banks serving as depositories and the city. This point will be referred to again in the discussion of the proposition to reduce the number of depositories and in reference to the establishment of better credit relations with the banks of the city.

fore, not available to him for guidance in handling his cash. These are now daily received at the chamberlain's desk and serve as an index to prospective requirements. Frequent communication between the comptroller's office and the chamberlain's office also makes possible arrangements of the cash to suit the proximate demands on the city treasury.

All of the foregoing is important, because, as previously explained, all checks are cleared through one clearing account. This clearing account is replenished as requirements demand from over one hundred deposits used as reserve accounts. Unless the accruing demands are carefully watched, there will be a tendency either to overstock the clearing account to the disadvantage of the depositories and the loss of the higher rate of interest paid by reserve depositories, or to make sudden and unforeseen withdrawals on these depositories to meet unexpected demands.

Clearing and Collecting Accounts

For the purpose of local convenience, it is necessary to have a bank of deposit in each of the five boroughs of the city where the collecting officers of the city government may daily deposit their funds at the close of business. The designation is regarded as highly desirable by the banks, for not only is there distinction and profit in receiving city funds, but a definite balance continuously remains as a deposit. In Brooklyn, the rivalry for the designation was so pronounced that to overcome the appearance of favoritism two collecting banks were designated and arrangements made which would effectively divide the business between them.

To compensate the banks for the work performed by them in receiving collections and making payments, it is customary to leave on deposit a considerable sum of money. Just what this sum should be had apparently never been determined. Tardiness in transferring funds received by the collecting banks to the central clearing bank for disbursement or for redeposit in reserve banks paying higher rates of interest would redound to the advantage of the collecting banks.

In the present administration we have adopted the rule of setting a certain percentage of the capital and surplus as the amount which would be left on deposit with the bank in compensation for work performed. This rule has been applied to all the collection accounts, including that of the city's main clearing bank. It is impossible, of course, to operate this rule with exact precision because of the fluctuations in receipts and payments. In the case of the clearing account the amount of the deposit must be increased to provide for exceptional demands, but the definite aim is to have the account maintained at $5,000,000 at the close of each day's transactions. In the other collection banks, the Peoples' Trust Company and the Kings County Trust Co. in Brooklyn, and the Corn Exchange in Richmond, Queens and The Bronx, a balance of from 5 to 10 per cent. of the capital and surplus is maintained to compensate the banks for their services. The value of stability is shown by the fact that we have received on two of the accounts interest at the rate of $2\frac{1}{2}$ per cent. since the plan was inaugurated.

Scattered Custody of City Funds

Various city officers are trustees of public funds. Thus, the police commissioner is trustee of the police pension fund, the fire commissioner of the fire pension fund, and the charities commissioner of the bastardy fund. The comptroller as trustee of the teachers' fund and as the recipient of security deposits of bidders on contracts receives annually large sums which he deposits to his account in banks selected by him.

At the beginning of this administration it was found that there was no uniform arrangement with the banks for these several classes of account, and that the same bank would pay varying rates of interest on different accounts of city money deposited by different city officials. A further complication of the banking arrangements of the city results from the fact that the chamberlain, as trustee of court funds, is required to deposit such funds in banks designated by the state comptroller. These banks are required to pay interest on such accounts at the rate of $2\frac{1}{2}$ per cent. per annum for New York county funds and 3 per cent. for other counties.

A condition of confusion thus existed which handicapped the city in effecting businesslike and satisfactory arrangements with the banks serving as depositories for the city's main funds. In this as in many other matters the city deals with a single question through a number of agents responsible for part of the problem instead of through one wholly responsible agent.

It is absurd, of course, that there should not be a single treasury of the city responsible for all its funds and conducting all negotiations with respect to these funds in banks. Here again is another case of patchwork, incoordinated charter-making which is the most prolific source of city government confusion and inefficiency.

City Borrowing

The city is a stupendous borrower. It borrowed $552,426,193.94 in 1913 and $406,059,858.64 in 1914. Its loans are made in the form of revenue bonds and corporate stock notes sold day by day through brokers to banks, insurance companies, private investors and, prior to the war, to the foreign market.

City securities are the most available and attractive form of short term investment in the market and are of conspicuous merit for the short turnover of funds. In recent years, with the growth in volume of city borrowings and with the introduction in the New York City market of similar short term securities issued by private corporations, New York brokers have developed a foreign demand for city tax warrants or revenue bonds and bills. It was because there were outstanding in the European market $80,000,000 of these short term notes falling due in the months of September to December, 1914, inclusive, that it was imperative for the city to arrange for the payment of this loan on the most favorable terms then obtainable for the protection of the city's credit.

The city's borrowings are made in anticipation of tax collections and in anticipation of bond sales. In 1914, $148,000,000 were in the former class, and $141,000,000 in the latter class. Tax borrowings are made necessary by reason of the fact that taxes are not payable until May of the year to which they apply, and then only for 50 per cent. of the levy, the balance coming due in November. The city might greatly reduce its borrowings if it were feasible to move back earlier in the year the first tax payment date. The present semi-annual payment was instituted through legislation obtained by Comptroller Prendergast in 1911. Prior to that time all taxes fell due in October. It is now merely a question of the respective convenience and ability to pay interest of the city and the taxpayers generally. The time is not far off when taxes will, in part at least, be paid at the beginning of the fiscal year. A further shifting of the tax date is not now contemplated, and therefore it will be necessary for the city to continue to borrow considerable sums of money.

When the city was confronted with the raising of the $100,000,000 loan, it was compelled to ask the help of the commercial bankers of the city. In the financial arrangement 122 banks in the city subscribed their proportionate share of the loan, and agreed to pay 80 per cent. of their subscription in gold in case gold was necessary for the redemption of foreign obligations. Several of the larger banks in the city entered into the arrangement reluctantly, because deposits had been withdrawn from them under the rule in operation since the first of the year, due to the fact that rates of interest offered by them were less than rates of interest offered by other institutions. These banks are among the so-called Wall Street banks, and are customarily underwriters of large security flotations.

In conference with the comptroller, the mayor and the chamberlain, it has been proposed in their behalf that the city enter into some arrangement with the large banks whereby they will always stand ready in times of emergency to finance the city as it was financed in the case of the $100,000,000 loan. It was further suggested in their behalf that in return for deposits made with them at 2 per cent. interest, they assume the moral obligation as bankers to find funds for the city when it is unable to obtain such funds more advantageously from other sources.

In ordinary times private bankers and bond brokers are able to loan funds to the city because investors are seeking immediate investment. In troubled times investments are shut off and cash seeks the banks and commercial depositories. It therefore becomes necessary in times of stringency to call upon the accumulations of banks of deposit for cash which would normally be obtained from private banks and brokerage houses. This condition may be mitigated by the operation of the new Federal Reserve Law, for under this law the reserve banks may purchase city securities. The position taken by the banks is that as they are accustomed to accommodate their private depositors in accordance with the volume of their business and the steadiness of their patronage, so in a similar way they would be prepared to accommodate New York City.

A working arrangement of this kind between the city and its depositories has for some time been in force in the city of Buffalo, where arrangements are entered into annually and are expressed in definite written contracts.

In Buffalo the banks agree to advance to the city, from time to time, such sums as may be required, specifying, however, in the agreement, the aggregate amount that such loans may not exceed, unless the banks shall later consent to advance a greater amount. The city agrees to repay the amount so advanced with interest at the rate of $4\frac{1}{4}$ per cent. per annum.

Summing up, the proposal is to obtain the good will and moral support of the principal banks of the city by designating them as city depositories and depositing funds with them at rates of interest which shall not vary but be maintained at 2 per cent. in consideration of their standing behind the city of New York in stressful times as well as prosperous times. Such an arrangement if made must involve the joint action of the comptroller and the chamberlain, for under the law the comptroller is solely responsible for making loans and the chamberlain solely responsible for the distribution of deposits.

The foregoing proposal in private business would seem to be wholly sound and a policy of good management. The question as to whether it is a proper arrangement for a public institution such as the municipality warrants further consideration. In the first place, there is a limited tenure of office on the part of public officials. The policy cannot be continued from administration to administration except as it justifies itself as a good business expedient. The obligation of the banks cannot be enforced, should it turn out when crises occur that they have no funds to loan. At the very time that the city is in need of such help the banks will be in the least favorable position to offer it.

Judging by past experience, both in the case of the $100,000,000 loan and in the case of loans made in the 1907 panic, the city would be required to pay adequately for the accommodation by the banks, for banking is not philanthropy but a business for whose management directors are responsible to stockholders, and city loans as well as other loans must be placed upon a business basis.

Because of my own strong conviction that the comptroller as the officer responsible for negotiating loans should be free to develop and utilize the borrowing facilities of the banks of the city, I have stated to him orally and in writing that I would be prepared to accept interest rates of 2 per cent. if a credit arrangement could be made with the banks paying this rate. It may not be generally known that certain of the larger commercial banks decline to pay more than 2 per cent. interest on any account. Their prestige and the volume of their deposits makes it unnecessary for them to do so. In these large banks depositors are often large borrowers. Interest payments on deposits, therefore, are a secondary consideration to large commercial depositors who have frequent occasion to borrow. Is the city in the same position? If it is, a deposit of city funds conforming to the usual commercial practice would entitle it to loans from four to five times the amount of the deposit. An ordinary commercial borrower, though he pay interest on his entire loan, is customarily obliged to leave on deposit during the period of the loan from 20 per cent. to 25 per cent. of the sum borrowed. On this deposit he generally receives no interest from the bank. Is it wise and necessary for the city to establish its relations with the banks on a commercial basis, with the exception that it would receive 2 per cent. on its balances? These balances, of course, in normal times, would be made up of revenue collections, taxes and loans from sources other than the commercial banks. The acceptance of 2 per cent. instead of higher rates obtainable would be justified on the principle of paying insurance against stringency occurring in times of crises or financial disturbance. In normal times, the city would borrow from sources outside the commercial banks. If the city is in a position where it must insure itself against inability to borrow in a tight market or in the face of a crisis, then it would be justified in taking this insurance in the form of lower rates of interest paid on city balances. The arrangement need not be permanent provided alternatives are developed.

In eleven months of the year 1914, despite the fact that in four of these months balances were cut down to sub-normal, the additional earnings were $114,041 over 1913 (excluding the interest earnings on the $100,000,000 loan, due to the fact that it is not customary to have so large a deposit for so long a period). This sum would represent the cost of insurance against inability to borrow in a disturbed or panicky money market.

It is merely a question of time when the city will further reduce the necessity for borrowing funds by shifting back the date of tax payments. The bankers themselves have obtained an agreement with the city in connection with the $100,000,000 loan for cutting down long term borrowings for improvements. The cost of these improvements under this arrangement is gradually to be included in the annual tax budget. According to this plan, after 1917 the city will not be obliged to borrow except in anticipation of taxes and for financing those expenditures which will result in self-supporting facilities, such as docks, water supply and railroads. For this group of bonds there will always be, except in great crises, a favorable market.

If other borrowings are reduced in the manner indicated, the relationship of the banks may be put entirely on the basis of adequate payment for deposits received, these, as previously stated, being in the nature of loans from the city to the banks.

Development of a Popular Market for City Bonds

A further possible alternative to the arrangement proposed is the development of a broader credit basis for the city. There has been frequent discussion of popular subscription loans. This discussion has related chiefly to the purchase of long term securities which are now to be cut down under the arrangement between the present board of estimate and the bankers, as above stated. There has been no public consideration of the exceptionally attractive form of investment represented by short term securities. It has occurred to me that possibly some such plan as the following might be developed.

The rates on the city's short term loans range from $2\frac{1}{2}$ per cent. to 6 per cent. The average savings bank rate is $3\frac{1}{2}$ to 4 per cent. Interest is not paid on savings bank deposits unless they are retained for three months. Interest is paid for each day on city securities. Large sums, upon which only 2 per cent. interest is paid, have been deposited in the Postal Savings banks in New York City since January 1st, 1914. Would it be feasible for the city of New York to make arrangements with the various banks in the city to place on sale continuously city short term securities in denominations of $10 and multiples thereof? The banks which are the fiscal agents of the city, as a portion of their obligation assumed as city depositories and in consideration of arrangements made with respect to interest paid on city deposits, might serve as trustees of funds paid into them on account of purchases of city securities. As required, the city would issue certificates for revenue bonds or corporate stock notes to the bank in amounts required to cover the subscriptions received from the public. As the revenue bonds and bills would be redeemed through the collection of taxes, the city would substitute corporate stock notes or corporate stock itself in denominations acceptable to small investors.

Under this plan depositors would be able first to buy short term obligations of the city, and second, to accumulate sufficient funds to purchase long term bonds. The city on its part would be developing a wider market for its securities and thus gradually put itself in a more advantageous position to deal with banks in times of stress.

In this connection it may be pointed out that one-half of the recent $100,000,000 loan was resold to the investing public, the amount available to the public for investment being subscribed two and one-half times. Whether some such plan as I have here outlined is feasible cannot be determined until a trial is made. There are, of course, arguments that may be advanced for and against its feasibility.

Reducing Number of Depositories

Separated from the foregoing consideration of credit relationships is the suggested reduction of the number of city depositories. The arguments advanced in favor of such reduction are:

    1—Greater simplicity in handling funds.

    2—Maintenance of more substantial balances in the remaining depositories.

    3—Removal of competition among banks for city deposits.

    4—Confining city deposits to banks which are in a position substantially to assist the city in making loans.

    5—Relief of the larger banks from the competition of smaller banks willing to pay higher rates of interest to obtain city funds.

My own judgment is that there should not be considered as city depositories banks with a capital and surplus less than $500,000, for in such cases the amounts of deposit are insignificant and the relationship is one purely of patronage and assistance to the bank. There is no countervailing advantage to the city. Within this limitation deposits should be made either on the basis of the rate of interest offered or on the basis of credit accommodations afforded, along the lines discussed above. For security and in support of the business activities of the various sections of the city, it is in my judgment appropriate that the city should maintain as large a number of depositories as is compatible with good business and efficient management.

Chamberlain as Trustee of Court Funds

On January 1st, 1914, there was in the custody of the chamberlain, as trustee, the sum of $4,529,000. These funds are cared for in two ways, first, by deposit in banks designated by the state comptroller (where they are secured by state bonds given into the comptroller's custody by the depository banks), and second, by investment.

On trust fund deposits the banks are required to pay $2\frac{1}{2}$ to 3 per cent. Each fund must be kept separate, not only on the books of the chamberlain, but on the books of the bank. There were 7,500 such separate funds on January 1st, 1914. The largest deposit in a single bank, $200,000, represented 720 funds.

These trust funds may be withdrawn from deposit only on the order of the court or of the state comptroller or for investment. During 1913 the withdrawals aggregated $2,500,000. All transactions in reference to trust funds are under continuous audit by representatives of the state comptroller's office.

Since January 11th, 1911, all investments are required to be in the form of city or state bonds. Prior to that time the chamberlain was permitted to invest in real estate bonds and mortgages. On January 1st, 1914, the chamberlain held 104 such mortgages, all of which represented loans made prior to May, 1910, except one mortgage paid in under a court order in 1912.

Requirements in respect of the custody of trust funds are laid down in the Code of Civil Procedure and in the regulations promulgated by the state comptroller. The rules of the state comptroller, as well as an order of the Appellate Division prohibiting the investment of funds in mortgages, presented a difficulty at the outset of my administration which arose from the fact that the term of trusteeship of the funds invested in mortgages does not coincide with the mortgage period. In order to continue the mortgage it has always been the practice in the chamberlain's office to transfer to the account of the mortgage new funds or uninvested old funds, as funds previously invested in mortgages were withdrawn by court order.

On submitting these facts to the state comptroller a waiver was obtained of the regulation prohibiting the investment of new funds pending such time as the chamberlain was able to dispose of all invested mortgages. The year 1914 was, moreover, an unfavorable year for liquidating mortgages. On January 1st, 1914, I found $1,200,000 invested in mortgages representing 104 separate loans. Of these 104 mortgages, 94 representing $823,000, were past due, and only 10 mortgages, representing $377,000, had not yet matured. These unmatured mortgages were executed in 1910. Overdue mortgages ran back as far as 1857. I found that five mortgagors were in arrears in the payment of interest and taxes. I found that my predecessor had foreclosed a mortgage on property located at 237 East 103d Street in the amount of $25,000, and that this property was being administered by the chamberlain for the benefit of the invested funds. In every case where there were delinquencies, I sought to protect the invested funds by insistently urging the mortgagors to make payments of arrears and to liquidate a part or all of the principal, if possible. In five cases this proved unsuccessful and foreclosures became necessary, representing property assessed at $111,500 and mortgages aggregating $79,800.

The foreclosures during the period were as follows:

	Mortgage	Assessed Valuation	Result of Sale
522 Stone Ave., Brooklyn	$9,000.00	$10,000.00	Satisfied
5719-21 Second Ave., Brooklyn	5,700.00	8,000.00	Bought in to protect mortgage
5723 Second Ave., Brooklyn	6,600.00	9,500.00	" "
497-501 East Houston St	22,500.00	41,000.00	" "
921 St. Nicholas Ave	36,000.00	43,000.00	" "

In each case the procedure in respect of foreclosures, as well as other mortgages in the custody of the chamberlain, was carefully discussed with Presiding Justice Ingraham of the Appellate Division of the Supreme Court, First Department, and his advice as well as the advice of the corporation counsel obtained as to their disposition.

As is generally known in real estate loan circles, real estate loans are not considered safe when they exceed 65 per cent. of the value of the property. On the basis of assessed valuations I found that 25 mortgages aggregating $650,900 exceeded the 65 per cent. limit. Therefore, through the courtesy of the comptroller, I immediately obtained an appraisal of all mortgaged properties on which we held mortgages of $10,000 or over by the real estate expert in the department of finance. In every case where the mortgage was overdue or the appraisal indicated an unsafe margin, steps were taken to bring about a satisfaction of the mortgage or reduction of the principal. In consequence, during the year 1914 mortgages to the amount of $57,000 were satisfied and payments on account in the amount of $4,500 obtained.

The investments negotiated in the year 1910, which will fall due on various dates in 1915, are peculiarly unsatisfactory, as the following statement will show:

Property	Amount of Mortgage	Assessed Valuation	Percentage Mortgage to Assessed Valuation	Finance Dept. Valuation	Percentage Mortgage to Finance Dept. Valuation
309 E. 121st St.	$15,000.00	$14,000.00	107	$15,000.00	100
326 E. 26th St.	17,000.00	20,000.00	85	20,000.00	85
1143 First Ave.	18,000.00	20,000.00	90	21,000.00	86
568 W. 173d St.	36,000.00	39,000.00	92	41,000.00	88
*921 St. Nicholas Ave.	36,000.00	43,000.00	84	40,000.00	90
1435 Madison Ave.	45,000.00	48,500.00	93	45,000.00	100
36 Convent Ave.	50,000.00	55,000.00	91	58,000.00	86
39 W. 17th St.	70,000.00	75,000.00	92	60,000.00	117
454 Broadway	75,000.00	68,000.00	110	75,000.00	100
**133-135 Greenwich St.	123,000.00	150,000.00	82	135,000.00	91
1125 Eastern Parkway, Brooklyn	15,000.00	19,500.00	77	24,000.00	62
	$500,000.00				

* We were obliged to foreclose on this property in 1914.
** This mortgage was made in 1910 and was due in 1913. It has been impossible to collect.

With respect to these, owing to the condition of the real estate market, my immediate purpose is to effect a reduction of principal where satisfaction cannot be obtained, and to ensure the prompt payment of all interest, tax and other charges.

Foreclosures would probably result in loss in most cases, and would increase the real estate holdings of the chamberlain, which is undesirable. I am submitting periodical reports on these transactions to the state comptroller and to the Presiding Justice of the Appellate Division of the First Department so that every step taken may be fully discussed and the judgment of all public officers interested in the transaction obtained.

A good deal might be said regarding the impropriety of these investments, but it will be futile to do so now. Suffice it to say that it was the particular mortgages falling due in 1915 which resulted in the rule of the state comptroller and the order of the Presiding Justice of the Appellate Division in 1911 that the chamberlain make no further investment of trust funds in mortgages. In almost every case the investment was of poor quality and indicated a lack of proper regard for the interest of the trust beneficiaries.

A word should be said for purposes of record regarding the method of administering the property which we have been compelled to foreclose.

237 *East* 103d *Street*—This mortgage, foreclosed in 1912 by Hon. Robert R. Moore, was for $25,000, against an assessed valuation of $31,000. The property consists of two stores and 15 apartments. The rentals in 1914 aggregated $2,400, and expenses and repairs $1,301.87, leaving a net income of $1,098.13, or 4 per cent. on the original investment.

497-501 *East Houston Street*—The first mortgage, held by the chamberlain, was for $22,500. The second mortgage, wiped out by the foreclosure, was for $3,000. After prolonged efforts to obtain response to his obligations on the part of the mortgagor, this property was foreclosed in 1914. It is a brick building used for various manufacturing purposes at the time of foreclosure. During the process of foreclosure it was seriously damaged by fire, the fire loss being covered by insurance.

In this case, as in all other foreclosures that we have had, we were the sole bidder at the sale. After careful examination by experts, and on advice from the Presiding Justice of the Appellate Division of the First Department to whom a full statement of facts was presented, I am having this property placed in first class condition for use as a loft building. It is estimated that the income to be derived from this building will give $3\frac{1}{2}$ per cent. to 4 per cent. return on the investment. This, of course, is problematical. This disposition of the property, however, was the only possible disposition under the circumstances, as no alternative of sale or lease on satisfactory terms could be developed.

The plans for the repairs of this property as well as the execution of the work are under the supervision of the superintendent of public buildings and offices in the borough of Manhattan. The efficient coöperation of the borough president's office will enable the chamberlain to effect repairs at low cost, and make available to him efficient agents skilled in building work without expense to the beneficiaries of the trust. This assistance and similar assistance obtained from the borough president of Brooklyn is a notable illustration of the coöperative spirit prevailing among city departments. I wish to acknowledge my indebtedness in this regard to Borough President Marks and to Borough President Pounds, who at all times have been most helpful.

921 *St. Nicholas Avenue*—The mortgage was $36,000 on an assessed valuation of $43,000. This property is an apartment house with 10 apartments. It was in fairly good condition at the time of the foreclosure. I have had this building placed in good repair, and have increased the number of tenants, and with continued success in securing tenants should be able to obtain a 4 per cent. return on the money invested.

5719-23 *Second Avenue, South Brooklyn*—The mortgage was $12,300 and the assessed valuation $17,500. This property had been permitted to fall into extremely dilapidated condition at the time of foreclosure due to the carelessness or the inability of the mortgagor to maintain it in suitable repair. Before satisfactory tenants could be obtained it was necessary to reconstruct the building. This was done with the coöperation of the borough president of Brooklyn, whose representative prepared plans for and supervised the repairs, thus effecting a very considerable economy and obtaining the highly competent attention of experts with which, of course, the chamberlain's office is not equipped.

As a result of the repairs made on this property, a much better grade of tenants has been obtained, rentals have been increased and we believe the property will produce this year a net revenue of $3\frac{1}{2}$ per cent.

133–5 Greenwich Street—In this case I found a mortgage of $123,000 on property assessed at $150,000. The mortgagor was in arrears for $11,000 for interest and taxes. After repeated conferences and urging, I obtained a stipulation from the mortgagor that the arrearages would be liquidated on certain specific dates, because it seemed unwise to attempt foreclosure on a property where the margin of equity was so narrow. In this case the obligation was lived up to practically as agreed upon except the liquidation of a portion of the principal. This is now again promised. The investment, therefore, is in very much better condition than when it came into my hands.

So far as possible it will be my purpose to avoid foreclosures. The practice of the office has, for years, been to continue mortgages past maturity where interest and taxes and other charges are promptly paid. This is advantageous, for the rate of interest on these mortgages is higher than the income which could be produced if foreclosures were insisted upon. Notwithstanding this fact, because of the order of the Appellate Division and the rule of the state comptroller, I am insistently urging the mortgagors to liquidate their obligations and shall continue to do so as long as the trusts remain in my hands.

Bond Investment of Trust Funds

In order to increase the earnings on trust funds not invested, I endeavored to withdraw from the depository banks all funds or portions of funds which might feasibly be invested in city securities. During the year I purchased for the benefit of trust funds $919,025 of city securities at current interest rates, ranging from $3\frac{1}{2}$ per cent. to 6 per cent. As mortgages are paid, partly or wholly, the proceeds so obtained are invested in city bonds.

In addition to city securities and mortgages held by the chamberlain, there have been turned over to him various other securities by court order which aggregate in book value $176,934,596.40. All but $4,150 of these securities are worthless in actual fact, but must be retained until they are disposed of by direction of the court.

On January 1st, 1915, the following were the trust funds held by the chamberlain in banks and in investments:

Bonds and mortgages	$1,085,446.89
Corporate stock	365,000.00
Revenue bonds	707,025.00
Miscellaneous stocks and bonds	4,150.00
Real estate	114,445.20
Cash in banks	1,510,117.46
	$3,786,184.55
Miscellaneous securities (no market value)	$176,930,446.40

Payment of Witnesses and Jurors

Payments of witnesses and jurors are made by the chamberlain on rolls prepared by officers of the court. These disbursements are not audited by the comptroller in advance of payment. The chamberlain accepts the certificate of the court clerk as conclusive evidence of the service performed by the juror or witness, except to the extent of checking the summonses or subpoenas to the rolls. In 1914, 54,000 jurors and witnesses were paid a total of $630,000, an increase of 25,000 in number and $275,000 in amount since 1905.

Prior to 1914, it was customary to require claimants for witness fees to call at the chamberlain's office for payment. In order to promote the convenience of the public and to make unnecessary personal attention to a large number of persons calling at the office, I instituted the practice of mailing checks to witnesses. This procedure has greatly simplified the work and has both promoted the convenience of the public and reduced the confusion prevailing in the office.

Bail Funds

The final class of transactions with which the chamberlain's office has to do is the custody of bail funds. The chamberlain's office receives for the five boroughs the cash bail paid into court in criminal and civil actions. In 1914 the aggregate receipts of bail funds in criminal cases were $800,000. During the time that they are in the custody of the chamberlain they are deposited in banks, drawing interest at 2 per cent. Inasmuch as this custody is for indeterminate periods, it is not the practice of the chamberlain to invest these funds. Interest on them accrues not to the bailors, but to the city of New York.

Internal Reorganization

The following chart shows the organization of the chamberlain's office. The deputy chamberlain is in charge of the administrative details of the office, which are voluminous and require his entire and continuous attention.

In order to place in charge of the actual signing of the warrants a responsible officer instead of a subordinate clerk as was heretofore the practice, I requested the establishment of the position of chief warrant clerk at $4,000 per annum, the title having previously been exempted from competition. This position I filled by the appointment of the former deputy chamberlain, who had over five years' experience in the office. All warrants and checks now pass through his hands, are subject to his scrutiny and are signed by him for the chamberlain.

The average daily number of warrants and checks drawn is 850. So long as action is required by the chamberlain in respect of these warrants, I deem it important that such action receive the continuous attention of a highly competent officer equipped to act with discrimination where any question presents itself with respect to the regularity of the transaction.

I abolished one exempt messengership, transferring the work performed by the former employee to a messenger whose salary is paid out of the mortgage tax collections under authorization of the state comptroller.

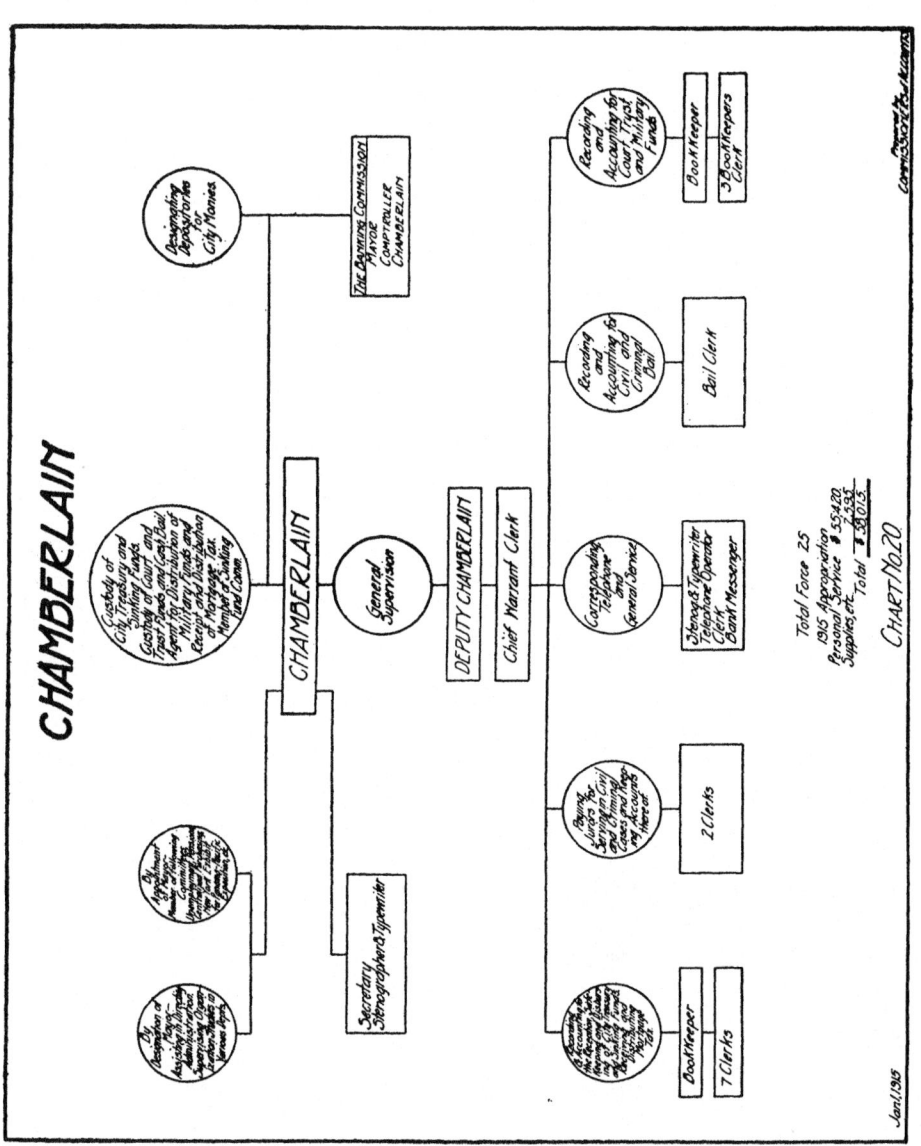

To the deputyship I appointed a certified public accountant of special qualifications in municipal work and training and ability in office organization and management.

The office of secretary was converted into an important working position, but the salary reduced from $3,000 to $2,000. The present incumbent has had years of training in municipal work, and not only performs the secretarial duties, which are extensive, but supervises the stenographic work and takes confidential and report dictation.

I have asked that another exempt clerkship, of which a woman has been the incumbent since May 1st, 1900, be classified and placed in the competitive service.

An additional clerk and an additional stenographer were appointed, both out of the competitive class.

I have done away with five exempt positions heretofore used for political rewards.

All these changes have resulted in increased efficiency in the office.

With all these changes the budget allowance for the office has been reduced from $63,943.40 for 1914 to $58,015.00 for 1915. Within this amount, in conformance with standards established by the bureau of standards, I have increased the salaries of employees long in the service and whose work is of an important character, in an aggregate amount of $1,170.

It may be well in this connection again to call attention to the fact that the cost of the office in 1914 was twice offset by the increased earnings under the new plan for distributing deposits instituted and previously described in this report.

It is not necessary to refer, except incidentally, to readjustments in accounting records and filing system, better office layout which resulted from the removal of the office to the new Municipal Building, and improvement in equipment which has been effected and which facilitates the efficient performance of the business of the office.

In all of this work I have had the most cordial coöperation of the comptroller. The office is now in close coöperation with other divisions of the department of finance, as it should be, and its functions are performed in harmony with those general fiscal transactions of the city which are under the comptroller's supervision.

Routine and Regulations

To govern all the functions of the office I have had prepared a descriptive routine of all transactions which are a part of the chamberlain's duties. In this way it will be possible for those who succeed me in responsibility for this work to have, on taking office, a definite description of the details of the work done and how it is done, and to have available at all times for reference a record of work methods. This procedure was prepared from a survey made by myself of the work of each subordinate, subsequently amplified by a description by the subordinate himself of methods pursued by him.

This description, after being modified in such particulars as seemed desirable to obtain more efficient practices, was then developed into a standard procedure.

Sinking Fund Commission—Its Merger with the Board of Estimate and Apportionment Recommended

Ex-officio, the chamberlain is a member of the sinking fund commission of which the other members are the mayor, the comptroller, the president and the chairman of the finance committee of the board of aldermen. The sinking fund commission under the charter has control of the sinking funds for the redemption of the city's debt and has jurisdiction over city property not in the custody of specific departments. It has, in addition, specific jurisdiction over the leasing of dock property, the execution of leases for the use of private property for city purposes, and the revision of assessments for public improvements on property used for religious, charitable or educational purposes.

Early in 1914 I had an analysis made of the transactions of the sinking fund commission to show their character. 40 per cent. of these transactions related to the making of leases, 11 per cent. were authorizations for the sale of city property at auction, 12 per cent. were cancellations of assessments, and the remainder related to various miscellaneous minor functions. As the volume of these transactions grows it becomes more and more necessary for the members of the sinking fund commission to rely upon the investigation of their agents. It so happens that the agents who report to the commission are the agents who report to the members of the board of estimate and apportionment on the transactions of that important board. The majority of the votes of the sinking fund commission, namely, those of the mayor, comptroller and president of the board of aldermen, also represent the majority votes in the board of estimate and apportionment.

As a simplification of the machinery of government I have previously made to you a recommendation which I now reaffirm—that the functions of the sinking fund commission be transferred to the board of estimate and apportionment. Many of these functions are mere survivals of an earlier time when the individual members of the commission were able to give personal supervision to all the details of city business. An illustration of this condition was a practice to which I called your attention earlier in the year and which thereafter was discontinued, namely, the fixation of the signatures of all members of the sinking fund commission to vouchers drawn by the dock commissioner in the use of corporate stock for dock construction purposes. The theory on which this was done was that the sinking fund commission, which is required to approve the requests of the dock department for funds to develop city-owned waterfront property, should also approve the specific expenditures in pursuance of corporate stock funds actually authorized. Obviously, the members of the sinking fund commission had no detailed knowledge of the transactions involving these expenditures, and relied wholly on the judgment and action of the dock commissioner. In the case of every other department, expenditures of a similar character are made by the head of the department, subject only to the audit of the comptroller and periodical review by the commissioners of accounts.

The transfer of the sinking fund functions to the board of estimate would mean merely an occasional lengthening of the calendar of the board of estimate and exclusion from consideration of these matters of the chamberlain and the chairman of the finance committee of the board of aldermen. In the suggestion that there be such an amalgamation, the present chairman of the finance committee concurs.

The following is a detailed statement of an analysis of sinking fund commission transactions in 1913 and a summary of board of estimate transactions. It will be seen that the total transactions of the sinking fund commission numbered 986 as aginst 6,188 of the board of estimate. The number of sinking fund meetings was 28 as against 52 of the board of estimate.

ANALYSIS OF BUSINESS COMING BEFORE THE COMMISSIONERS OF THE SINKING FUND DURING 1913

	Section of Charter Controlling †	Number of Items	Officer Passing on Matter Previous to Action by Commissioners	Percentage
*Leases..........................	217	392	Comptroller	40%
*Transfer of property and funds..	205-205a	75	Comptroller	8%
Refund of moneys.............		75	Comptroller	8%
*Auction sales.................	205-220	105	Comptroller	11%
*Cancellation of assessments, etc.	221a	114	Comptroller	12%
*Quit claims...................	205	44	Comptroller	4%
Space in municipal building....		15		2%
Communications..............				5%
*Dock leases...................	219	40	{Dock Dept. to Comptr.}	4%
*Highway rights on water dept. lands....................	205	9	Comptroller	1%
Fixing salaries...............		1		
Redemption of city debt......	207	4	{Compt. to Bd. Est. & App.}	
Issuance of corporate stock...	187-219	23	{Compt. to Bd. Est. & App.}	2%
Hearings.....................		18		2%
Fixing rate of interest........	169-205	1		
Authorizing purchase of bonds	213	1		
Payment for armory work....	217	5		
Establishing high water mark.	205	3		1%
Rescinding grants of franchises.		1		
Liquor tax license............		4		
Space, Bronx courthouse......		6		
		986		100%

* Matters unrelated to business of Board of Estimate and Apportionment.

† It will be noted that these sections of the charter cover nearly all the activities of the commissioners including bond issues and custody of sinking funds, and to transfer these functions to the board of estimate and apportionment will require charter amendments in each instance. There is no legal impediment that the legislature cannot overcome provided distinctly legislative functions are given to a legislative body.

SUMMARY OF BUSINESS COMING BEFORE THE BOARD OF ESTIMATE AND APPORTIONMENT DURING 1913

Class	Number of Items
Public Improvements	
Resolution changing map	26
Engineer's financial statements	23
Miscellaneous	23
Manhattan	238
Brooklyn	1,129
Bronx	328
Queens	505
Richmond	77
Franchise matters	215
Financial (items of annual budget omitted)	3,624
	6,188

NUMBER OF MEETINGS DURING 1913

Month	Sinking Fund Commission	Board of Estimate and Apportionment
January	2	4
February	2	4
March	3	6
April	5	5
May	2	6
June	3	5
July	2	3
August	—	1
September	2	3
October	2	8
November	3	4
December	2	3
	28	52

There is no sufficient reason for maintaining a sinking fund commission as an independent body merely for the purpose of the custody of sinking funds. As a matter of fact, the custody of funds is in the hands of the comptroller. While each new sinking fund commission makes an inventory of the holdings of the sinking funds, and thereafter theoretically assumes custody of them, the actual custody remains with the comptroller. The inventory might quite as well be made by the board of estimate. Much more effective control would be obtained by a periodical audit of sinking funds by the commissioners of accounts, and the publication of its findings.

```
HJ        New York (City)
9389        Bureau of city
.N44      chamberlain.
A23
1915        The reorganization
          of the office of
          chamberlain
282954
```

Printed in Dunstable, United Kingdom